# Kitchen Memories

George,

Mix food family and love for Great Kitchen Memories

# Kitchen Memories

## Recipe Paintings with A Taste of Art
## Brenda Erickson

All content is the property of the Brenda Erickson, Recipe Paintings, Inc., PO Box 294, Round Pond, Maine 04564, 207-529-5367, RecipePaintings.com. Original paintings, Prints or Books may be obtained from the author.

Kitchen Memories is a total Maine Production with Maine Art, Maine Design and Maine Printing.

Library of Congress Control Number: 2010930684
ISBN 978-0-9767321-6-7

**Rocky Hill PUBLISHING**

13 Lilac Garden Road, Damariscotta, Maine 04543 USA
207 380 6074 • RockyHillPublishing.com

Printed by Penmor Lithographers, Lewiston, Maine

To My Mother
Norma Dunning Martin

# Acknowledgement

I want thank all of the families who have shared their Recipe Painting™, their recipe and their stories.

I would also like to mention the many families for whom I have painted recipes. I apologize for not having room in the book. It was difficult making the choices as each recipe I've painted has been meaningful and I love them all.

Special thanks to my friends, family and following businesses with whom I've worked directly:

Ron and Belinda Fletcher, Fletcher Gallery
Cynthia Finnemore Simonds, TV Chef of 'Fresh and Flavorful' and cookbook author
Al Trescot, Rocky Hill Design
Don Carrigan, WCSH 6 TV, 207 Show
MPBN's Great TV Auction
Caren Helm, Pizzazz Pottery
Kate's Homemade Butter
Rod Williams, Williams Creative
Randy Miller, Newcastle Chrysler
Bull's Point Lobster, Round Pond
Bill & Elaine Shuman and SCORE
Michael Good Designs
Chef Rick Hirsch, The Anchor Inn
The Inn at Round Pond
Lynne Leavitt, Maxwell's Pottery
The Damariscotta Pumpkinfest

Bobby Ives, The Carpenter's Boat Shop
Georgia Manzo Joachim, "A Taste of It All"
Granite Hall Store
Supplies Unlimited
Smiling Hill Farm
Bakewell Cream
Cold River Vodka
Round Pond Lobster

In recognition of the oysters in the Damariscotta River, I've included "Belly Up to the Oyster Bar."

# Forward

I will never forget the day that Brenda was talking about her paintings of recipes and said, "I don't care if this ever goes anywhere, I just want to have fun doing it." And now here I am, a couple years later, writing a forward for my good friend and fellow artist's book filled with just a few of the many recipe paintings that she has created. I met Brenda and her husband Bob when they first purchased one of my own paintings. Due to my own history of being a recognized artist and also just living down the road, Brenda has come to jokingly call me her "unofficial art director." However, Brenda has never really needed an art director.

Brenda has been involved in painting since she was a teenager in high school. She has taken many art classes and most recently worked under the instruction of several prestigious watercolor instructors of Maine. Being a creative cook herself, Brenda then took a very natural step and combined her watercolor talent and culinary experience and has created a very special combination, "Recipe Paintings." We all have those memories of that special recipe of Aunt Emma's Chocolate Cake with her secret ingredient or Nana's Seafood Stew that just made everyone go ahhh! "Kitchen Memories" has all that.

"Kitchen Memories" is a finely illustrated book sharing family heirloom recipes for the kitchen or the coffee table. It is a tasteful arrangement of wonderful family recipes passed down through the years that are sure to bring smiles to all. A great book to have for culinary memories or beginnings and certainly an artistic coordination for your most discriminating house guest to browse through.

Brenda's watercolor illustrations have fantastic attention to detail, color and composition. Seeing the illustrated final cooking result will make you want to run to the kitchen and try the recipes yourself. Or better still, get her to paint your favorite recipe for all to see and enjoy for many years to come.

Brenda, your recipe paintings took off like wild fire. Now the book … fantastic drawings and paintings and memories.
I wish you the best. You deserve it.

*Ron Fletcher*

(Your unofficial art director)

# Forward

Imagine the aroma of crusty bread baking; the first bite of a fresh-from-the-oven, gooey chocolate chip cookie; the sight of a perfect apple pie cooling on the windowsill …

When you think back to your first memory of food - where does it take you? Sometimes it's a smell that transports us into grandmother's kitchen or the sight of a family culinary heirloom, like the antique breadbox from mom's pantry, that reminds us of meals past. Turning back time, even for the span of a single dinner, is a gift to be cherished.

Family recipes are treasures. Each one connects us with a memory. When I was growing up my mother was always baking. She had cookbooks as a guide but everything was done by feel. I remember her standing behind me, our hands moving together in the fold, press, lift, turn of graceful kneading. Whenever I make bread I am reminded of her. I can see mom at the floury kitchen counter. The air would be permeated with the warm, tangy smell of rising bread. I never could wait until the loaves cooled before snitching a steamy moist slice and slathering it with butter; watching as the liquid gold filled every lacy curve. I can smell it right now. She learned early on to make two loaves for every one she needed; knowing that once it was done the kids would be in the kitchen before she closed the oven door.

I believe recipes should be shared. Meals are meant to be a joining of people and pleasure. The table is a place to come together; to find each other; to celebrate family and create new traditions.

Brenda has captured the essence of these special memories in still life. When art marries flavor the results are more than the sum of their parts. The recipes in her paintings are a snapshot, a moment in time; preserving family recipes new and old, some with very specific ingredients; allowing us to turn back the clock once more. With Brenda's artistic, epicurean portraits, families are able to recreate the dishes that anchor them to milestones in their lives.

We cook together, sharing laughter in the kitchen. We eat together, bringing the same joyful spirit into the center of the table. Brenda's recipe paintings simply and beautifully achieve exactly that. They capture the delicious joy in a special memory and preserve it, to be shared by many, forevermore.

*Cynthia Finnemore Simonds*

# Introduction

Cooking and art are similar in many ways. Essentially they are both creative activities. You learn how to paint or cook either by formal training or by enjoyment and experience. Both take planning, preparation and practice. Understanding when they are complete takes even more experience. These are the physical aspects of cooking or painting.

There is also the joyful art of cooking and what I call 'A Taste of Art.' That involves spending time with others to know what they would enjoy eating or seeing. Although the preparation time can be lengthy, the time spent in the kitchen with family and friends is a warm and wonderful experience. It is similar to the time I spend and the conversations I have with people about what is important to them about the recipe I am to paint. Certainly reaching the final stage; serving the meal or delivering the painting is most exciting. That first taste; that first look. There is a period of silence as everyone absorbs the moment. Then comes the happiness, sometimes tears, remembering with excitement. The stories bubble out and the love flows.

I started cooking with my mother as most people do with the usual cookies and cakes. With time I worked up to simple meals. As a child, I remember the responsibility of making scrambled eggs for my father's dinner while my mother went to an evening meeting. I remember the smiles and commotion in the kitchen as family members made final preparations for holiday meals. Everyone seemed to be working in unison and harmony in our tiny kitchens. To keep me from getting in the way, I was allowed to sit on a stool next to the stove and stir the gravy. As I grew older, I learned not only how to prepare elaborate recipes, but how to make a delicious meal with ingredients on hand.

My art has followed a similar path. I've enjoyed drawing and painting all my life; learning from experience and taking the occasional class as time permitted. In the 90's, I took the opportunity to study seriously under Maude Olsen, a marvelous instructor from South Bristol, ME. Through her I learned my love of still life, which developed into the illustration of recipes. My first painting was Salsa and my second was Maine Lobster Bake. Both came to me in those wonderful 3AM thoughts and dreams. Thus Recipe Paintings™ was born. My friends, neighbors and family have supported and encouraged my artwork. Cynthia Finnmore Simonds and I met as her books were being published, her television cooking shows were beginning and my Recipe Paintings™ were growing. We have much in common, starting with a simple recipe. Ron and Belinda Fletcher of Fletcher Gallery in New Harbor, ME have gently guided me through the art world maze. And through everything, my husband Bob has been all of the above. He encourages, supports, guides, teaches, believes and loves.

*Brenda*

# Contents & Equivalents

### Equivalents

1 tsp = 1/3 tbsp

2 tbsp = 1 fluid oz

4 tbsp = 1/4 cp or 2 oz

5 1/3 tbsp = 1/3 cp

8 tbsp = 1/2 cp or 4 oz

16 tbsp = 1 cp or 8 oz

2 cps = 1 pt

2 pts = 1 qt

4 qts = 1 gal

# Salsa

| | |
|---|---|
| 4 | Tomatoes, diced |
| 1 | Sweet onion, diced |
| 2 large | Fresh jalapeno peppers, seeded and minced |
| ¼ cup | Fresh cilantro, chopped |
| ¼ cup | Fresh squeezed lime juice |
| 1 clove | Garlic, minced |
| 2 tbsp. | Olive oil |
| 1 tsp. | Salt |
| ½ tsp. | Freshly ground pepper |

In a medium bowl, combine all ingredients. Cover with plastic wrap and let stand at room temperature for 1 hour to allow the flavors to blend.

B.Erickson

This is my first Recipe Painting™. I have made this recipe many times while living in Arizona, the land of salsa. We had moved to be close to my husband Bob's family. It is best made with fresh, homegrown vegetables. Today the painting hangs in my brother-in-law's kitchen. Richard is one of the best southwestern cooks and it's an honor for him to have it.

# Guacamole

2 ripe Avocados
1/2 cp Salsa
1 fresh Lime

Mash avocados; mix with salsa
Add lime juice if desired.
Season with salt and pepper.

B. Erickson ©

This is a recipe that I never measure. I don't think you can do anything wrong as long as you don't over power the ripe avocado.

# Craig's Blue Cheese Dip

1 tsp pressed garlic    1 tsp Worcestershire Sauce
½ tsp dry mustard    ¼ tsp Tabasco
¾ tsp black pepper    1 cp sour cream
⅛ tsp white pepper    3 cp mayonnaise
¾ tsp onion salt    ½ cp buttermilk
¼ cp Balsamic Vinegar    12 oz Blue Cheese

Whisk together garlic, mustard, peppers and onion salt. Add vinegar, Worcestershire and Tabasco. Add sour cream, mayonnaise and buttermilk. Fold in Blue Cheese and chill. Will keep for one week. Makes 6 cups

B. Erickson

Craig is not a gourmet cook, but like the rest of us, when he comes to your home for a meal, he likes to bring something to share.

Many times he brings his special dip with crackers and vegetables or uses it as a dressing on a salad.

# Bruschetta

1 lb ripe Tomatoes
2 sm cloves minced Garlic
Salt and fresh Pepper
10 Basil leaves, chopped
¼ cp diced Green Onion
¼ cp diced Green Pepper
⅓ cp Olive Oil
1 loaf French Baguette Bread
Olive Oil for brushing

Combine tomatoes, garlic, salt, pepper, basil, onion, pepper and oil. Let stand at room temperature 1 hour. Slice bread, brush with olive oil, and toast under broiler until golden brown. To serve, place vegetable mixture and juice on bread and press down lightly.

B. Erickson ©

Bruschetta is a favorite of mine to make in the summer with fresh-from-the-garden ingredients. I was painting this recipe when Don Carrigan interviewed me for the WCSH6 207 Show.

Since this Recipe Painting™ has been so good to me, I shared it with others by donating it to the Maine Public Broadcasting Great TV Auction.

## Nana True's Scramble

1 1/4 lb Margarine
3 tbsp Worcestershire sauce
1/2 tsp Ground red pepper
1 tbsp Celery salt
1 tsp Garlic salt
Mix all in saucepan and melt

In large pot mix:
7 oz Cheerios
12 oz Wheat Chex
7 oz Rice Chex
1 bag Pretzel sticks
1 can Mixed nuts
1 can Peanuts

Pour melted ingredients over dry ingredients and stir well. Spread in two cookie sheets and bake in 225° oven for 3 hours. Stir each half hour to ensure even cooking. Cool and serve. This is a family favorite during the holiday season.

B. Erickson ©

Becky asked me to paint her mother-in-law's Scramble recipe for her husband Bob's birthday. She said Christmas wouldn't be Christmas without Nana True's Scramble. She selected and bought all the ingredients she wanted in the painting, then had to explain to her husband why she was buying Scramble ingredients in October. She came up with a story and we surprised Bob.

14

# Pizzazz Dipping Oil

1 Pizzazz Pottery Garlic Grater
1 T grated garlic
1 T Italian parsley
1 T minced basil
1 t thyme
1 t oregano

1 t black pepper
1/2 t sea salt
1/4 t red pepper flakes
1 C chopped parsley
1/2 C olive oil
Fresh bread for dipping

Blend all ingredients except garlic and oil.
Grate garlic in bowl; add oil and spices.

B. Erickson ©

I met Caren at a show in Wells, Maine where she was selling these wonderful garlic graters along with her many other beautiful pieces of pottery. We illustrated her garlic grater and recipe in this painting.

### Pesto

1 1/2 cp fresh basil leaves
1/4 cp pine nuts
3/4 cp grated Parmesan cheese
2-4 cloves garlic
3/4 cp olive oil

Blend all ingredients.
Toss with hot pasta
and serve.

B. ERICKSON ©

It's always exciting when the basil plant reaches maturity for picking. Some people see a delicious dinner. I see not only a delicious dinner, but also a beautiful painting.

# "Ma" Kellner's Piccalilli

1/2 Bushel green tomatoes
4 Red hot peppers
3 Bell peppers
4 lbs Onions

Cut and layer vegetables - Cover with a handful of salt - repeat to use all vegetables - Cover pot and leave overnight - Drain off excess liquid - do not squeeze.

Add 1 1/2 qt vinegar, 3 lbs brown sugar, 1 tsp each cinnamon, paprika and cloves. Put pickling spices (whole) into cheesecloth bag and drop into mixture - cook slowly 3 hours.

B. Erickson ©

After I completed Nancy's painting, I asked her if the recipe was difficult to make. She said she had never made it and didn't know of anyone in the family who had, except for her father who made it once.

He also made an absolute mess in the kitchen. She added that just seeing the painting helps her recall the taste of the piccalilli and the warm memories of both her father and grandmother.

17

# Neena's Happy Hour

Neena's time is a special time for relaxing and happy chatter, whether coming back from the beach, a shopping spree or just a brief visit. Simply pour a glass of wine, (or two), slice some cheese and crackers and enjoy the Williams' girls for good cheer and memories.

I met Rod after the WCSH 6 TV, 207 Show. He introduced me to Kate's Homemade Butter. We have worked together and kept in touch ever since.

He asked me to paint Neena's Happy Hour for his wife, Carolyn and their two daughters. The three glasses represent the three of them sharing time at the end of a busy day.

# Bud's Punch

Mix
2 cp Orange Juice
2 cp Cran-Raspberry Juice
2 cp Pineapple Juice
1 cp Dark Bacardi Rum
1 cp Light Bacardi Rum

Place pineapple slice, orange
  and cherry in glass.
Top with splash of grenadine.

B. Erickson ©

Bonnie asked me to paint her Uncle Bud's punch recipe. She loaned me the glasses and described how this was her uncle's favorite drink.

I can only imagine him making these delicious drinks and serving them to his family and friends.

# Randy Miller's White Cosmo

2 parts Vodka
1 part Cointreau
White Cranberry juice
1 squeezed Lime

Shake with ice.
Strain into chilled Martini glass.

B. Erickson ©

Randy serves his cool and refreshing Cosmos with white cranberry juice.

# Appletini

2 oz vodka
1 oz sour apple liquor
splash lemon juice

Mix vodka and liquor in shaker with ice.
Strain and serve. Top with splash of
lemon juice and garnish with green apple
wedge.

B. Erickson ©

I painted Bud's Punch and had such fun with it, even before testing, that I decided to do a series of drinks. Appletini was my first. Naturally I had many volunteers to help test the recipes!

### Maine Martini

Cold River Blueberry Flavored Vodka
Orange Twist
Fresh Maine Blueberries

Chill Vodka, garnish with orange
twist and blueberries.

B. Erickson ©

Cold River Vodka is made in Freeport, Maine with Maine potatoes. Their Blueberry Vodka has wild Maine blueberries added.

It's always exciting to paint Maine ingredients. This is a simple, sophisticated and elegant drink.

# Atomic Fireball

1 part Dr. McGillicuddy's Fireball
1 part Crown Royal

Serve over ice.
Sip slowly and let the
fire burn.

B. Erickson ©

This is Doug's favorite drink. It has a kick so I added, "Sip slowly and let the fire burn."
Great on a cold, rainy evening in Washington State.

## Renewal Manhattan

1 oz Southern Comfort
2 oz Sweet Vermouth
2 Maraschino cherries
Comfortable old couch

Fill glasses with ice; add Manhattans.  Put your feet up.  Get comfortable on the couch.  Share experiences of the past and look for new beginnings. Talk, laugh, cry and love being together.

(Oooooooooooh!)

Donna and Eddie met again, after many years. Their recipe says it all.

## Craiger's Manhattan

3 oz Seagram's 7 Whiskey
1 oz sweet vermouth
dash of cherry juice

Measure into a shaker filled with ice.
Shake, strain and pour into glasses
filled with ice. Garnish with a cherry.

This is Craiger's specialty drink. It hangs above his bar next to a sign that quote's his dad: "A Clean Bar is a Happy Bar."

# Shrimp Chowder

2 tbsp butter
1/2 large onion, chopped
1 celery stalk, chopped
2 tbsp red pepper, chopped
1 cp water
1 tbsp flour
1 1/2 cp cubed potatoes
1/2 lb Maine Shrimp, peeled and uncooked
2 cups whole milk
1/2 cp Monterey Jack Cheese, shredded

Saute onion, celery and pepper in butter. Add water and potatoes, sprinkle with flour. Cook 15 min. Add shrimp, cook 1 min. Add milk and cheese. Blend, heat but do not boil. Serve with fresh, crusty bread.

In Maine, shrimp are fished in the winter. Fishermen either drag or trap the shrimp and the shrimp are sweet and tender. I buy my shrimp locally at Bull's Point Lobster in Round Pond.

# MaryLou's Fish Chowder

1 1/2 lb haddock fillets
1 med onion, chopped
1/3 cp. + 3 tbsp butter
4-5 potatoes, cubed
2 cp. boiling water

3 cp milk or cream
1 cp evaporated milk
3 tbsp flour
2 tsp salt
1/2 tsp pepper

Sauté onions in 1/3 cp butter until golden, sprinkle with 3 T flour. Add potatoes, salt, pepper and boiling water. Stir well. Arrange fish fillets on top. Cover and simmer until potatoes are tender. (about 20 min.) Add milk, evaporated milk, 3 T butter. Heat - don't boil. Let cool. Flavor improves if heated and cooled a couple of times.

B. Erickson ©

Everyone who visits Maine at MaryLou and Jack's home enjoys MaryLou's Fish Chowder. Fish Chowder is a family recipe that has many variations, but this one is our favorite.

One secret ingredient is the evaporated milk. The other is the memories of the wonderful times shared with MaryLou and Jack.

# Japanese Fried Rice

An original recipe by Normand St. Marie

| | |
|---|---|
| 1 large glass of white wine | 2 slices boiled ham (1/4-in thick) |
| 2 cups cooked white rice (long grain) | 2 eggs, fried well-done |
| 4 large carrots | 1/4 cup vegetable oil |
| 4 large onions (plus six green onions) | 1/3 cup soy sauce |
| 4 large green peppers | salt and pepper to taste |

Cook the rice, the day before. Cut fresh vegetables into 1/4 inch cubes. Cut ham and eggs into 1/2 to 3/4 - inch pieces. In large cast iron skillet, heat oil. Add carrots; cook 7 to 10 minutes on a medium-high fire. Add peppers, onions and seasonings. Cook until near done, stirring. Don't overcook Push vegetables to one side; add rice. Break up the rice and vegetables. Occasionally toss vegetables with rice with a spatula. Add soy sauce and mix with the vegetables. The rice will tend to stick if it is overcooked; remove, lower heat and return. Stir in ham and eggs. Taste; add soy sauce if necessary. Remove from heat and drink the wine - you deserve it!

B. Erickson ©

Nathan asked me to paint this recipe for his Mother. Normand is Nathan's pépère . When we were setting up the painting, he sent me a photo of his pépère in the kitchen with a chef's hat on. I really appreciate it when I can put a face to the recipe. It becomes very real to me.

# Elva Goddard's New England Succotash

2 cups shellies (October beans)
2 in. cube of salt pork, well slashed
3 medium-sized ears of corn
1/2 teaspoon salt

Cover beans, salt pork and salt with water. Cook about 1 to 1 1/2 hours (until just about done), over low heat after bringing to a boil. Add corn which has been cut from cob (scraping cob to get all the milk). Continue to cook 1/2 hour longer, stirring frequently to prevent sticking. The secret of the goodness of this dish is in keeping sufficient liquid in the beans during the entire cooking period so that there is ample "pot liquor" to be served with the succotash.

B. Erickson ©

Barbara asked me to paint this recipe for her family and explained that when she was growing up as a child during WWII on a very limited income, each child was allowed to choose what was served for dinner on their birthday.

This was her favorite. I've since talked with her brothers about their birthday dinners and they recall all the recipes and exactly how their Mother prepared them.

Don Carrigan is the reporter who interviewed me for the WCSH 6 TV, 207 Show. Don is known for measuring the snow depth on his grill in the winter. The Memorial Day weekend before interviewing me for the show, Don and Rob Caldwell were cooking Don's Burgers on the show.

I've often laughed about what the neighbors must have thought as I was cooking burgers on the grill at 8:00 AM, preparing for this painting. About half way through the painting, the burgers were in the refrigerator when my hungry husband, Bob, saw them … fortunately there were extras!  Bob agrees, Don's Burgers are delicious even when they're heated up.

# Don's Burgers

Fresh Ground Beef, 90% Lean
Steak Sauce
Dry Onion Soup Mix

The key to a great burger is great ingredients, and just the right amount of time. 90% lean cooks faster, but tastes better, so keep watch.

Add flavor and juiciness with a little steak sauce and dry onion soup mix. Mix it up and squeeze it down, but go easy here, too much just makes a mess. You could also use a little Worcestershire sauce or chopped onions. Make a generous size patty. Not too thick, it will be easier to cook evenly.

Cook on high or medium high heat on the grill. Don't squash flat while cooking. This will force the juice out, and leave a less tasty burger. Grilling time depends on the grill and your taste. Practice.

I think cheddar cheese makes the best cheeseburger. After all, if you can't taste the cheese, what's the point? Toast the roll. Go cold if you're in a hurry, but a toasted roll with a little butter is the crowning touch.

Condiments are up to you, but a well cooked burger is tasty just by itself.

B. Erickson ©

# Polish Pierogies

**Filling**
5 lbs. potatoes (White
   Rose or Yukon Gold)
24 oz. extra sharp white
   cheddar cheese
5 small onions (chopped
   and sautéed in butter)

**Dough**
4 cups flour
2 eggs
5 T sour cream
4-6 T vegetable oil
3/4 cup water

Filling: Peel and boil potatoes. While potatoes are hot, mix in cheese and onions. Let cool.

Dough: Make mound out of dry ingredients and make a well in the center. Place wet ingredients using only 4 T of vegetable oil in the center. Knead well with hands or use dough hook on mixer. Add remaining oil as needed to reach right consistency. Divide dough into 4 balls and keep unused portions wrapped until ready to roll out.

Roll dough out thinly, then cut 4-inch circles. Place desired amount of filling off center on each circle of dough. Fold over and seal with crimper, fork or fingers by moistening edge with water and putting pressure on edges for a firm seal.

To cook: Drop pierogi into gently boiling water. Cook for 5 minutes. Remove gently with strainer spoon and brown in butter or margarine on griddle. Divide portions evenly and serve with sour cream.

Kirstie's family makes this recipe on Christmas Eve. In the painting we used her Mother's grill. We also added "divide evenly..." because of a story she told me about a high school boyfriend not only eating more than his share, but also taking her father's last pierogie. That was probably the last date.

# Memere's Pork Pie

1 1/2 pounds ground beef
1 1/2 pounds ground pork
2 med potatoes (cook until soft
  then mash with salt and pepper)
1 tsp. ground clove (approx.)
1 1/2 tsp. cinnamon
1 small onion, diced and fried

Cover meat with water, add spices. Stir until
cooked. Drain excess water. Combine with onion
and potatoes. Bake in pie shell 350 degrees until
brown, about 45 minutes. Makes 2 pies.

B. Erickson ©

Kristen and Wendy always knew Christmas was right around the corner when Memere started baking her pork pies! "We remember going to visit Memere when she was in the middle of making the pies.

The whole kitchen was turned into a 'Pork Pie Factory.' We added a little of this and a little of that 'til it was just right. Memere always made sure she had enough 'special sauce,' as Dad called it…to put on top."

I met Elizabeth at a show in Wells, Maine. Several months later she called to discuss her Mom's meatloaf. She grew up with this recipe and now serves it to her family and friends. She described how her Mom made the meatloaf and after several sketches, we got the shape just right.

Some people don't understand why the shape of the meatloaf is so important since it is actually the ingredients that make the flavor. But when you look at your painting, it's the shape that brings back the memories of being a child, watching and helping to make the meatloaf, smelling it cooking with the baked potatoes and sitting at your special place at the table when it's served.

# Grandmommy's Meatloaf
### February 1964

1 can Campbell's tomato soup
1 1/2 lb ground beef
2/3 c. fine dry bread crumbs
1 egg
1/3 c. finely chopped onion
1 t. salt
generous dash pepper
1/4 c. water
1 t. horseradish

Mix thoroughly 1/2 c. soup with next six ingredients. Shape firmly into 2 loaves. Place loaves in shallow baking pan. Bake at 350 degrees for 40 minutes. Top with remaining soup, water, and horseradish. Bake 5 minutes more or until done.

B. Erickson ©

# Mom Aron's Most Excellent Deluxe Salad Dressing

½ cp Heinz Apple Cider Vinegar
1 ½ cp Wesson Oil
4-6 Cloves Garlic, cut in half
2 t Salt
1 t Sugar
No Tabasco
1 t Pepper
1 + t Paprika

Mix all ingredients except Tabasco. Continue adding ingredients as dressing is used. Second batch better than first, and so on….

This is a great recipe with a funny story. It is one of my early recipes and I painted it for our son-in-law, Jim, just before a visit to California where they live. Unfortunately, just as I finished the painting, I realized his recipe didn't call for Tabasco! It's good either way.

## Georgia's Italian Meatballs
### from
### A Taste Of It All, 2008

1 1/2 lb. ground sirloin or chuck steak
1/2 lb. ground pork
1 1/2 tsp. salt; 1 tsp. freshly ground black pepper
2-3 sprinkles of cayenne pepper
3 large eggs
1 1/2 tbsp. dried parsley
3 garlic cloves, minced
1/2 cp. Parmesan cheese, freshly grated
4 tbsp. olive oil
3-4 (1-inch thick slices of mealy bread (such as
   semolina) or coarse white bread, crust removed,
   or 3-4 English muffins
Skim milk for soaking bread
Imported Mozzarella cheese, 1/2 in cubes for
   center of meatball (optional)

B Erickson ©

Scott contacted me to paint Georgia's recipe. It's his favorite recipe from her new cookbook, "A Taste of It All."  After Georgia received the painting, I ordered her book and it's now one of my favorite cookbooks.

# Toot-a-Lings

Filling:
1/2 cp ground beef
1/2 cp ground pork
1/2 cp breadcrumbs
1 tsp nutmeg
1/2 cp grated Parmesan Cheese
3-4 eggs
Sauté meat. Add remaining ingredients.
Mixture should be sticky to hold into small balls.

1 large pot chicken soup
When soup is boiling, add Toot-a-Lings; cook 10 min.

Dough:
4 cps flour
6-8 eggs
Mix well and knead. Work in small portions.
Roll thin. Cut in small squares. Place filling in
center, fold into triangle, seal edges; bring
together two corners, seal.
Set on lightly floured platter.

P.Erickson ©

Lou and Paula make this recipe every Christmas Eve. It is Lou's mother's recipe and
the bowl and scoop are ones she used. Although she also rolled the dough, Lou
and Paula's children grew up using this pasta maker. At Christmas this year, each
child received a print and the traditional pasta maker.

# CANAL ZONE CASSEROLE

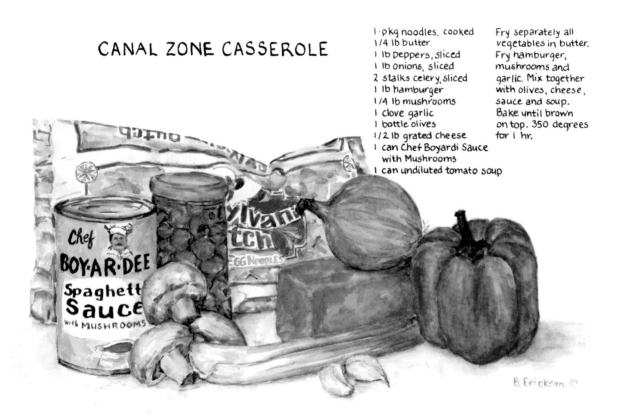

1 pkg noodles, cooked
1/4 lb butter
1 lb peppers, sliced
1 lb onions, sliced
2 stalks celery, sliced
1 lb hamburger
1/4 lb mushrooms
1 clove garlic
1 bottle olives
1/2 lb grated cheese
1 can Chef Boyardi Sauce
  with Mushrooms
1 can undiluted tomato soup

Fry separately all vegetables in butter. Fry hamburger, mushrooms and garlic. Mix together with olives, cheese, sauce and soup. Bake until brown on top. 350 degrees for 1 hr.

B. Erickson ©

This is my family's recipe. When painting this for my cousin Beverly, I researched the name and discovered that it was created in the 1920's by Johnny Marzetti, from the Marzetti Restaurant in Columbus, Ohio. Later it became popular in the Panama Canal Zone and then returned to the US in women's magazines in the 1960's when my family discovered it. Today there are many versions with many different names.

My mother would sauté the vegetables in butter, but today I microwave each separately making it nutritious as well as delicious.

## The Original Joan Carey Macaroni & Cheese

16 oz Creamettes Elbow Macaroni
3 tbsp butter
2 tbsp flour
1 tbsp Coleman's dry mustard
2 cups half and half
2 cups Kraft extra sharp
   cheddar cheese shredded
3-4 slices of Wonder bread torn
   in pieces for crust

Preheat oven to 350°
Butter a 13 x 9 casserole

Cook macaroni, drain, but do not rinse.
Melt 3 tbsp of butter, whisk and blend with
flour and mustard. Slowly add half
and half stirring constantly until thickened.
Place cooked macaroni in casserole
and pour sauce over macaroni mixing
until well coated. Combine cheese with
macaroni mixing together thoroughly.
   Cover casserole with bread.
   Drizzle top of casserole
   with butter. Bake for
   approximately 45 minutes.

B. Erickson ©

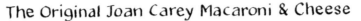

Joan raised and fed eight growing children with this rich and creamy, traditionally baked macaroni and cheese recipe. Each child remembers it fondly and now serves it to their children.

# Montine's Glorified Macaroni

1 - 8 oz. box elbow macaroni
1/2 cup bell pepper, chopped (optional)
1/2 cup onion, chopped
1 small jar chopped pimento
1 can cream of mushroom soup
3/4 cup mayonnaise
1 pound grated HOOP cheese (reserve 1 cup)
1 stick margarine or butter
Saltine cracker crumbs (about one sleeve)

Cook macaroni as directed on the box, drain and let cool. Mix next six ingredients in a large bowl and add cooked macaroni and 1/2 of the margarine, melted. Mix well and spoon into a greased baking dish. Sprinkle with reserved cheese. Melt remaining margarine and mix with saltine cracker crumbs and put on top of the cheese. Bake at 350 degrees until top is nice and brown.

G. Erickson ©

Margot asked me to paint her mother's Glorified Macaroni Recipe. She explained that Hoop Cheese is a southern cheese, similar to mild Cheddar. This recipe has been passed down three generations with Margot's son who now makes a variation with chicken. She also added that her mother always wanted her recipe to be submitted to a national women's magazine. It would have won an award.

## Spaghetti Sauce by Mom

1 large onion, chopped
Olive oil
3-4 cloves garlic, minced
Basil, dried
1 can tomato paste
3-4 cans water

1 large can chopped tomatoes
Pepper
1/2 cup red wine
1-2 tbsp sugar (approximately)
Italian sausage, if desired

In heavy, deep non-aluminum pot, cover most of bottom with olive oil. Heat. Add onion and lots of basil. Grind pepper into pan and let cook for five minutes or so. Add garlic; cook 1 minute. Add paste, tomatoes and water; mix well. Add wine and 1/2 of sugar. Bring to simmer; let cook. Taste; add more sugar if necessary. Italian sausage adds a nice flavor to sauce but is not necessary. Simmer until desired thickness. If you don't want to add wine use small amount of balsamic or red wine vinegar.

B. Erickson ©

Bob and I had fun setting up this painting for his wife Maggie. The spoon and pepper grinder sit on her counter. The wine bottle is representative of a recent trip, and the recipe book is one that Maggie and one of her daughters assembled with Mom's Recipes.

# Mary's Sauce
## A Papi Family Tradition Since 1953

Bone-in pork ribs and sweet Italian sausage
Meatballs
3 cans Pastene crushed tomatoes
2 cans tomato paste
1 whole onion peeled
3 cloves whole garlic, peeled
dried basil and parsley to taste
salt and pepper
a little sugar
red wine to taste, about 1/2 cup

Mary's Meatball's
3 lbs ground beef
2 eggs
1 cup Italian breadcrumbs
dried basil, parsley and
    garlic powder to taste
1/2 cup parmesan cheese
salt and pepper

Brown pork and sausage in extra virgin olive oil,
Remove from pot. Add all other ingredients.
Bring to boil. Lower heat and return meat to pan
and cook for 3-4 hours or until meat is very tender.
Remove meat and add meatballs to sauce. Cook
another 30 minutes. Remove whole onion and garlic
before serving.

Meatballs
Mix together and shape into balls. Fry in
olive oil.

Regina asked me to paint her mother Mary's recipe several years ago. Just a year ago Regina's sister called for another print as her son, Mary's grandson, needed a copy for his new home in Texas.

When Amanda's mother was a teenager, her mother showed her how to make this recipe as the first meal served to her boyfriend. Eventually, Amanda's Mom and Dad married. Because they were living as a one-income family with four daughters, this was a staple in their home. Amanda told me, that even when she was in college, her Mom always sent her back to school with a Tupperware container full of Mom's Spaghetti.

Now that Amanda and her sisters are married with children, the fourth generation, Mom's grandchildren call this dish "Grammy Pasta." Two of the daughters are married to Italian men who roll their eyes at the thought of garlic powder and tomato soup in a spaghetti sauce. We used Mom's pot, wooden spoon, jelly jar full of oregano and store brand ingredients just as Mom does. To me this is the ultimate family recipe, now being enjoyed for the fourth generation.

# Mom's Spaghetti
## (Grammy Pasta)

1 1/2 lb dry spaghetti
1 lb ground beef
2 tablesp oregano
1/4 tesp pepper
A shake or two of garlic powder

Small chopped onion
  (or 1 teasp or so of onion powder)
1 - 15 oz can of tomato sauce
4 cans tomato soup undiluted

Oil the bottom of a large, heavy pan. Saute ground beef and all flavorings together until beef is thoroughly cooked, stirring frequently. Then reduce heat to medium. Add tomato sauce and soups, stirring thoroughly. Gently bring to a boil, stir, lower heat, and simmer several minutes, stirring occasionally. Serve with approx. 1 1/2 lbs dry spaghetti noodles cooked and drained according to package. Serves 6

Pat asked me to paint her Mom's recipe, but said it would be a while before we could start since she had to get it into written form. It's among my favorites since it first says, "Go to Buddy's" for the Lobsters. Buddy owns one of the lobster pounds in Round Pond. Then, "...grate 'til you're tired of grating; that will be enough." Perfect. That's how a family recipe is told.

The other great story about this family recipe is that when the Shumans gather each summer on the Pemaquid Peninsula, the first question after everyone is settled is, "which night is Mom making the Lobster Casserole?" This year when they gathered, they checked to see how accurately Mom made her casserole.

# Mom's Lobster Casserole

(as described by Mom, aka Elaine Shuman)

Go to Buddy's and ask for culls. Use 1 less lobster than diners (depends upon size of lobsters and if you're buying whole lobsters or culls; use at least 4)

1 cup of rotini per lobster; at least 3 cups

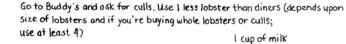

1 cup of milk

Grated sharp Cheddar cheese - grate 'til you're tired of grating; that will be enough

Butter

½ cup or more dry sherry (You can use any kind of sherry; I've even used Harvey's Bristol Cream)

Cook rotini until just tender; drain and rinse. Heat milk, season with salt and pepper and pour over rotini; stir.

Cut off a piece of butter and throw it in the pan - might be a half a stick. Sauté the lobster in the butter 3-4 minutes; add sherry.

Place a layer of rotini in a casserole. Spoon a layer of lobster over it. Sprinkle with cheese. Repeat, ending with cheese on top.

Bake at 350° until bubbly and melty.

B. ERICKSON ©

## Baked Stuffed Maine Lobsters Dubord

1 (16 oz) pkg milk crackers, crushed
4 (1 1/2 lb) Maine hardshell lobsters
2 cps butter, melted

juice of 1/2 lemon
salt and pepper to taste
1 tbsp garlic powder

Have chef at local fish market pick the lobsters. They should be swimming as aggressively as the chef would swim in the icy waters of Frenchman's Bay. Place crackers in bowl. Hypnotize lobsters by standing them on their heads with claws folded backwards and rubbing the topsides of their tails. After 30 seconds, lobsters will be ready for preparation. Quickly turn lobsters onto backs and hold by mid-sections with gloved hand. Insert knife into the head and down through tail, taking care not to cut through the back of the shell. Scoop tomalley and place in small bowl; discard entrails. Open body by reaching underneath and cracking shell. Place lobsters on a foil-covered baking sheet, sprayed with oil. Beat tomalley and crumbs lightly. Stir in seasonings. Add butter. Preheat oven - 350°. Pack lobsters with stuffing. Bake 45 minutes; serve with melted butter.

Dianne contacted me about her husband Dan's favorite Baked Stuffed Lobsters recipe that he makes on special occasions. We included the cookbook Maine-ly Good Eatin' in which Dan's recipe is printed.

# Maine Lobster Bake

Ingredients: 2 Maine Lobsters
1 lb. Clams
Fresh Corn

Directions: Cook lobsters, clams and corn accordingly. Add a pinch of salt air. Blend with the sound of laughter. Mix with great company and good cheer. Serve on a warm summer night.

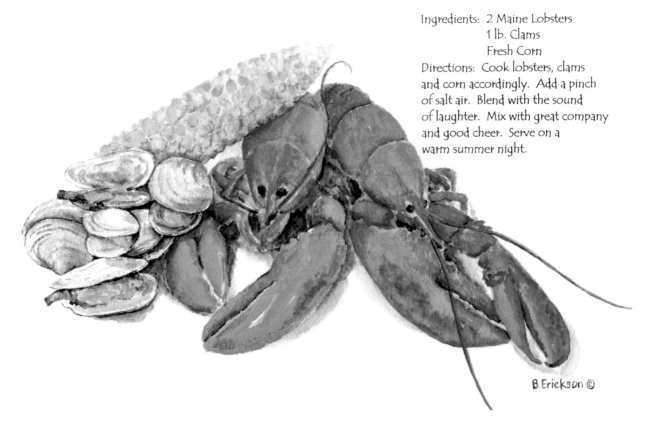

B. Erickson ©

This is one of my favorite paintings and hangs proudly in my home. The 'directions' came to me one night at 3 AM. Most people read this recipe and say those are the lobsters they ate last night … week … or summer.

Sharing time, laughter, friendship and love are what good recipes are all about.

# Boiled Maine Lobster

Bring a large pot of salted water to a rolling boil. Place lobsters in the boiling water. When the pot returns to a boil, start timing and continue to cook for 20 minutes. Serve with melted butter and lemon wedges.

B. ERICKSON

I paint many lobsters for my Recipe Paintings™. I cook each lobster to look at while I am painting. Until I looked closely at lobsters, I never knew how different each lobster looks.

# Maine Lobster Rolls

2 cups cooked lobster meat
2 tbsp mayonnaise
4 hot dog rolls

Toss lobster meat lightly with mayonnaise. Butter and grill hot dog rolls in a frying pan on medium heat. Fill rolls with lobster mixture and serve.

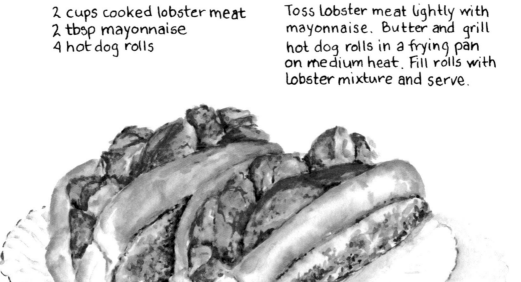

B. Erickson ©

A good Maine Lobster Roll is lobster and a little mayonnaise. Nothing more. Of course it needs to be served in a properly grilled hot dog roll, on a paper plate.

## Michael's Belgian Steamed Maine Lobster

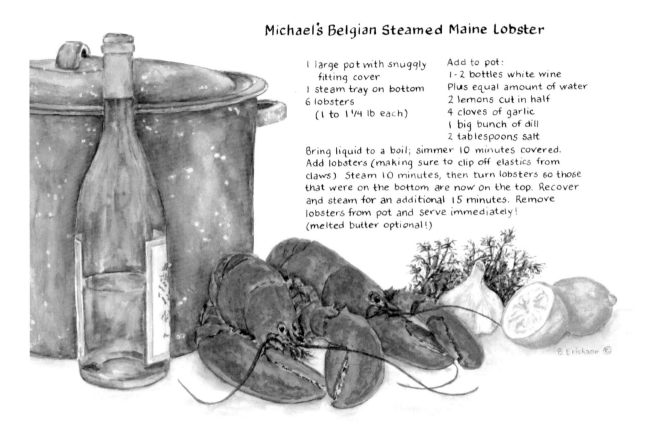

1 large pot with snuggly
   fitting cover
1 steam tray on bottom
6 lobsters
   (1 to 1¼ lb each)

Add to pot:
1-2 bottles white wine
Plus equal amount of water
2 lemons cut in half
4 cloves of garlic
1 big bunch of dill
2 tablespoons salt

Bring liquid to a boil; simmer 10 minutes covered.
Add lobsters (making sure to clip off elastics from
claws) Steam 10 minutes, then turn lobsters so those
that were on the bottom are now on the top. Recover
and steam for an additional 15 minutes. Remove
lobsters from pot and serve immediately!
(melted butter optional!)

B. Erickson ©

This is a recipe that jeweler Michael Good of Michael Good Designs in Rockport, ME serves to his friends and family. It is a traditional Maine lobster recipe with flavors inspired from his family's home country of Belgium.

# Broiled Haddock

1 lb Haddock
Olive Oil
Garlic, minced
Salt and Pepper
Paprika

Rosemary
Thyme
Parsley
Lemon

Blend olive oil and garlic. Brush oil on fish. Season with salt, pepper and paprika. Place fish in grill basket. Grill over hot coals for 8 to 10 minutes turning once. Remove from heat. Season with minced rosemary, thyme and parsley. Serve with lemon wedges.

When Libby was asked which is her favorite recipe made by her Mom, she said Broiled Haddock. This is how Jenny makes Broiled Haddock.

# Mom Townley's Clam Pie

5 large potatoes cut into small cubes
2 large onions chopped
2 bottles clam juice
1 pound chopped clams
8 dropped biscuits for topping

Precook potatoes and onions until partially cooked. Drain saving 1 cup of liquid. Heat clams and clam juice and combine with drained warm potatoes/onions/saved liquid. Drop biscuits onto warm potatoes/onions/clam mixture. Bake at 350° 1/2 hour or until biscuits are browned.

B. Erickson ©

This is a favorite of the Townley family. Larry and his sister Mary Lou remembered Mom's recipe with fondness and wanted to pass it on to future Townley generations. The original bowl was duplicated by a local potter for each of their two children. Before doing the painting, I asked if there was a special way to roll the biscuits for the topping. "No, this isn't a fancy dish, Mom just dropped the biscuits on."

## Anchor Inn's Italian Seafood Stew

| | |
|---|---|
| Onions | Red Pepper Flakes |
| Garlic | Black Pepper |
| Tomatoes | Clam Juice |
| Basil | Maine Shrimp |
| Oregano | Mussels |
| Thyme | Scallops |
| Parsley | Haddock |

Sauté onions and garlic. Add crushed tomatoes, herbs, peppers and clam juice. Simmer to blend flavors. Cook seafood in broth. Serve with warm garlic bread.

B. ERICKSON ©

The Anchor Inn is a fabulous restaurant near us in Round Pond, Maine. When I started this painting, I had to decide whether to paint the finished dish or fresh ingredients.

I decided to illustrate all the fresh herbs and seafood that make Chef Rick Hirsch's recipe so special. This painting now hangs at this popular Mid-Coast restaurant.

# Steamed Clams

8 pounds steamer clams       3 cloves garlic, peeled and sliced thin
   (Serves 4)                1/2 cp chopped fresh parsley
1/4 cp olive oil             1 cp dry white wine
                             black pepper to taste

Wash clams in large pan with running water. Watch for clamshells that are filled with mud. The clam has left home! Soak clams in fresh water for about 1 hour before cooking to complete cleaning.

Heat large soup pot, add oil and garlic. Cook for a moment and add remaining ingredients, including drained clams. Cover and bring to boil. Stir well once. Cover and simmer a few minutes until clams open. Discard any that do not open. (8-10 min.)

Stock in bottom, or nectar is wonderful. Serve it by the cup with a little freshly ground pepper on top.
Serve clams with green salad, fresh bread and too much beer.

B. Erickson ©

This is a company dish for guests visiting Dennis and Pam. I had never had clams cooked with garlic, parsley and wine, however since I usually make each recipe that I paint to fully appreciate what I'm painting, I cooked the clams this way and they are absolutely delicious. You must always have crusty bread to sop up the delicious broth.

# Steamed Mussels

4 lbs mussels
4 cloves garlic, finely chopped
3/4 cp fresh parsley, chopped
1 cp white wine

Rinse mussels in cold water, discard broken or open mussels. In large pot, add mussels, garlic, 1/2 of parsley and wine. Cook 5 minutes or until mussels open. Stir in remaining parsley. Spoon mussels and broth in wide bowls. Serve with crusty bread.

B. Erickson ©

When I was growing up, no one ever ate mussels. Sometime in the 80's we were introduced to them and have been eating them ever since. Serve with a good bottle of wine and crusty bread. Ummmm.

# Easter Bread

made year round by Stevie
I consider this to be the best bread that there is.
It gives the family a quick breakfast.

**Combine (a)**
2 cakes yeast
½ cp lukewarm water

**Combine (b)**
1½ cups oatmeal
½ cup sugar
1 tablespn salt
½ cp shortening
½ cup raisins

3 cups scalded milk
7 to 7½ cups sifted flour
2 beaten eggs
½ cup sugar
3 tablespns cinnamon

Soften yeast in warm water (a)

Pour milk over (b) which have been placed together in large bowl. Cool to lukewarm. Beat in half the flour, beat in yeast and eggs. Add flour to make soft dough. Knead until smooth and elastic. Place in greased bowl, cover and rise until double, about two hours. Punch down, cover and rise again.

Divide dough into three parts; round each into a ball. Roll with rolling pin into rectangle. Combine cinnamon and ½ cup sugar. Sprinkle evenly over each rectangle. Roll up to form a loaf. Place in lightly greased bread pans with seam down. Cover and rise until double. Bake 350° for 40-50 min.

Cooking Hint: To keep milk from curdling when boiling, add a pinch of baking soda.

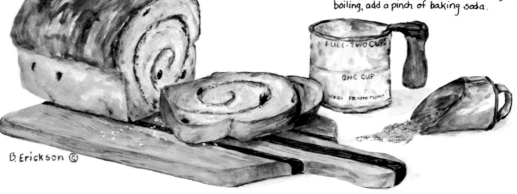

B. Erickson ©

Stevie made this bread when her family was young and growing. It has everything for a balanced breakfast on the run. We included her mother's two-cup sifter, a scoop her son made in industrial arts and the beautiful cutting board made for her by her husband Mac. Stevie also, reminded me what a small world this is, as the flour sifter was manufactured in the 1930's by Erickson of Des Moines, Iowa.

# Theresa Bicknell's Whole Wheat Bread

3 1/4 cp white flour
3/4 cp whole wheat flour
1 egg
1 tsp salt
1/4 cp sugar

1/4 cp molasses
2 pkg dry yeast
1 cp milk
1/3 cp warm water
1 tbsp shortening

Bring all ingredients to room temperature. Dissolve yeast in 1/3 cp warm water. Scald milk and add shortening. Cool slightly, add molasses, sugar, salt, dissolved yeast and egg. Stir in whole wheat flour and enough white flour to make a stiff dough. Knead for about 10 min and then put in a greased dish and allow to rise in a warm place. When almost triple in bulk (about 2 hours) punch or cut down; divide and make into 2 loaves. Let rise again (about an hour) and bake for 30 min in a 350° oven.

B. Erickson ©

Lynn's mother made this bread everyday when he was growing up in Vermont. He remembers clearly the smell of the bread baking when he returned home after school.

# Orange Muffins

| | |
|---|---|
| 1 orange | 1 ½ cp flour |
| 1/3 cp orange juice | 3/4 cp sugar |
| 3/4 stick butter | 1 tsp powder |
| 1 egg | 1 tsp soda |
| 1/2 cp raisins | 1 tsp salt |

Grate rind from orange and reserve. Discard pith, quarter and seed orange. In blender, mix rind, quarters, juice, butter and egg. Add 1/2 cp raisins and blend 5 seconds. Transfer to bowl. In another bowl, sift flour, sugar, powder, soda and salt. Stir flour mixture into orange mixture until combined. Divide evenly in buttered and floured muffin tins. Bake 400°, 15-20 min.

B. Erickson ©

Sally's family makes these rich, crispy muffins for special occasions. And now, so do I.

Biscuits

2 Cups sifted All Purpose flour

3 tablespoons granulated Sugar

1 tablespoon Baking Powder

½ teaspoon Salt

½ cup (1 Stick) Cold Butter cut up.

¼ cup milk

425° Oven

Pat or roll the dough out on a lightly floured board to about ½ inch thick, Cut 8 Biscuits

Place on Ungreased baking Sheet for 15 Min.

B. Erickson ©

Pam has many recipes from her Mum, Aurelia Gould, to choose for her Recipe Painting™. She chose biscuits because this is the recipe her Mum taught Pam's husband, Randy, to make. I asked Randy how his biscuits are and he assured me that his mother-in-law was a great teacher.

# Breda's Honey Cake

Oven 150°c for 3/4 hour
8 oz. self-rising flour
6 oz. honey
4 oz. butter
2 large eggs
pinch salt
6 1/2 x 7 1/2 inch tin

B. Erickson ©

Breda's family keeps the bees that make this award winning honey. They live in Ireland. Bonnie asked me to paint this for their daughter's wedding gift. It was an honor.

# Nana McCobb's Coffee Cake

1 cup sugar
1/2 cup butter or margarine
1 1/4 cup flour
1 rounding spoon baking powder

Mix flour, sugar and shortening with fingers. Add 1/2 cp milk, 1 egg. Mix cinnamon, brown sugar and nuts. Sprinkle on top.

Bake 350°, 30 min.

B. Erickson ©

Janet's family recipe is from her Great-Grandmother, Nana McCobb. We have three generations of dishes represented here. When Janet first saw her painting, her response was, "I can taste the coffee cake." Now her grandchildren are the sixth generation to enjoy it.

63

Corn Spoon Bread

2 slightly beaten eggs
1 8½ oz. pkg. Jiffy corn muffin mix
1 8 oz. can cream style corn
1 8 oz. " whole kernel corn, drained
1 cup sour cream
½ cup (one stick) melted margarine

Mix all together put in 9×9" pan. Bake 350° for 35 min or until lightly brown

B. Erickson ©

George's Mother has shared this recipe with many. In the painting, we used Gram's wooden spoon, recipe card and the box that her husband made. The brands of ingredients are the ones she would have used when visiting her granddaughter, Carole in Connecticut.

## Gram's Banana Bread

Sift 2 cps flour
1 tsp baking powder
1/2 tsp baking soda
1 tsp salt
Cream 1/2 cp butter, gradually add 1 cp sugar, cream well.
Blend in 2 large eggs, one at a time, beat well.
Add 1 cp mashed banana, mix well.

Blend in sifted ingredients. Pour into greased, 9x5x3 tin.
Bake 350°, 50-60 minutes.

B. Erickson ©

Banana Bread is a recipe that every family enjoys. Because I have painted several
different banana bread recipes, it was difficult to choose only one. This is Bonnie's
mother's recipe. She gave this painting to her son, making it Gram's Banana Bread.

# Blueberry Buttermilk Pancakes

| | |
|---|---|
| 1 cp flour | 1 egg |
| 1 tbsp sugar | 1 cp Kate's Buttermilk |
| 1/4 tsp salt | 1 1/2 tbsp melted Kate's Butter |
| 1/4 tsp soda | 1 cp Fresh Maine Blueberries |
| 1 tsp powder | Maine Maple Syrup |

Combine dry ingredients. Add liquids until flour is moistened. Gently mix in Blueberries. Drop batter by spoonfuls on lightly oiled griddle. Turn pancake when bubbles appear and bottom of pancake is brown. Serve with Kate's Homemade Butter and Maine Maple Syrup.

B. Erickson

Kate's Homemade Butter and Buttermilk make all the difference for these pancakes. Maine blueberries and Maine maple syrup add the final touch.

# Ruth's Blueberry Muffins
### Makes 2 dozen

2 cups Sour Cream
4 Eggs, beaten
1 cup Vegetable Oil
2 cups Sugar
4 cups Flour
1 tsp. Salt
1 tsp. Soda
2 tsp. Powder
2+ cups Blueberries
Mix with love.
Bake @375° for 24min.
Serve with coffee and tea.

B. Erickson ©

The Carpenter's Boat Shop was founded in 1979 by Ruth and Bobby Ives. Located in Pemaquid, Maine, it is an apprenticeship school and community for all people. Ruth served these muffins everyday at 10:00 AM from this muffin pan and tea from her teapot. Profits from the sale of this print go to Carpenter's Boat Shop in loving memory of Ruth.

# Blueberry Cake

Cream 1/2 cp butter, add 1 cp sugar, cream well
Add 2 eggs, one at a time
1/2 to 1 tsp nutmeg; 1 tsp lemon flavoring
Sift 1 1/2 cp flour with 2 level tsp baking powder
Add alternately with 1/3 cp milk
Add 1 1/2 cp blueberries, (lightly sprinkled with flour)
Mix. Pour into 9" square pan, lightly greased.
Sprinkle top with sugar. Bake 350°, 50 min

B. Erickson ©

There are so many wonderful recipes for blueberry season. Here is one of several Blueberry Cake recipes that I've painted.

3 C flour
1/2 C sugar
4 tsp baking powder
1/2 tsp baking soda
1/4 tsp salt
8 tbsp unsalted butter, chilled
1 tbsp grated lemon rind

3/4 C buttermilk
1 large egg
1 tsp vanilla extract
3/4 C blueberries

# The Inn at Round Pond
# Maine Blueberry Scones

Preheat oven to 400 F. Lightly grease baking sheets. In large bowl, stir flour, sugar, powder, soda and salt. Cut butter into flour mixture until you have coarse crumbs. Stir in lemon rind. In small bowl, stir buttermilk, egg and vanilla. Add buttermilk mixture to flour mixture. Stir to combine. Stir in blueberries. With lightly floured hands, pat dough into 2 8-inch circles on baking sheets. With a serrated knife, cut each into 6 wedges. Bake 20 min. until top is lightly browned and toothpick inserted in center comes out clean.

D. Crichton

Bill and Sue have the greatest Bed and Breakfast in Round Pond. Mary asked me to paint the blueberry scones as a gift to them for all the wonderful times they have shared as a family at The Inn at Round Pond. Sue helped me pick out Mary's favorite china for the painting.

69

# Apple Pie

2 2/3 cp flour
1 tsp salt
1 cp shortening
6 tbsp water

6 apples, sliced
2/3 cp sugar
1/4 tsp salt
2 tbsp flour
1/4 tsp cinnamon
1 1/2 tbsp butter

Pie Crust: Mix flour and salt in bowl. Cut in shortening until just blended to form pea sized chunks. Sprinkle with water 1 tbsp at a time. Toss lightly with fork until dough forms a ball. Divide dough into two parts. Roll to form two crusts.

Pie: Heat oven to 450°. Toss apples, sugar, salt, flour and cinnamon. Place in piecrust. Dot with butter. Top with crust. Bake 450° for 10 minutes. Reduce temperature to 350° and bake 45 min.

B. Erickson

Apple Pie is an American favorite. This is my mother's Apple Pie.

# Bonnie's Apple Pie

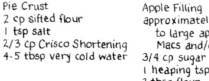

**Pie Crust**
2 cp sifted flour
1 tsp salt
2/3 cp Crisco Shortening
4-5 tbsp very cold water

**Apple Filling**
approximately 10-12 med
   to large apples
    Macs and/or Cortlands
3/4 cp sugar
1 heaping tsp cinnamon
2 tbsp flour
2 tbsp butter

Mix small amount of milk and butter.
Microwave to melt the butter. Brush over top crust.
Sprinkle with sugar. Bake 400° 50 min.

B Erickson ©

Bonnie likes to pile the apples high in her apple pie.

## Mom's Apple Pie

6 c perfectly cored and peeled apples,
   sliced 1/4" thick
2/3 c sugar
1/4 tsp nutmeg
1/2 tsp cinnamon

1/8 tsp salt
1 tsp lemon juice
1 tbsp butter

With all distractions behind her, Mom lovingly layers 6 cps of perfectly prepared apples in her famous beautifully rolled pie crust. She then carefully measures and sprinkles over the apples (which look like a work of art), sugar, nutmeg, cinnamon, salt and lemon juice. Then she tops this beautiful pie with pats of butter.

At this point, Mom neatly rolls the top crust and gently places it on the apples. She presses the edge with her fingers in a precise pattern Mom bakes this beautiful pie at 425° for 40-45 minutes for all of us to enjoy.

B. Erickson ©

Aunt Claire likes to neatly line up the apples before baking her pie. This is an all day project. She not only lines up the apples with precision, she smoothes them off and tops it with a beautifully rolled piecrust. Delicious!

# Merriam Family Camp Apple Pie

4-5 apples thinly sliced
2 tsp cinnamon          1 tbsp flour
1 tsp nutmeg            2/3 c white sugar
1/2 tsp salt            1/3 c maple syrup

Bring a pie crust and vanilla ice cream to camp. Pick your favorite apples at North Star Orchard. Peel and (thinly) slice the apples, add the remaining ingredients to the apples and stir to coat the apples evenly. Create your own personal flare for top crust. Bake at 400, first 35 min. w/tin foil, next 25 w/o tin foil.

Enjoy the pie and ice cream on the dock or in front of the wood stove.

B. Erickson ©

Jennifer told me the recipe and crust are not as important as picking the apples and eating the pie at camp, either at the end of the dock or in front of the wood stove. She is hoping this will be a family tradition carried on by her son, Tyler.

# Dina's Favorite Brownies

(Makes 24 - 2"
   square brownies)

1 cp (4 oz) Pecans or
   Walnuts chopped
   (optional)
1 1/4 cps (5 oz) Flour
1/2 tsp Salt
3/4 tsp Baking Powder
6 oz Unsweetened
   Chocolate, chopped fine
12 tbsp (1 1/2 sticks)
   Unsalted Butter
   (cut into six 1" pieces)
2 1/4 cps Sugar
4 large Eggs
1 tbsp Vanilla Extract

1.) With oven rack in middle position, heat oven to 325 degrees. Cut 18 inch length foil, fold lengthwise to 8" width. Fit foil into length of 13" X 9" baking dish, pushing it into corners and up the sides of pan; allowing excess to overhang pan edges. Cut 14" length foil and if using extra-wide foil, fold lengthwise to 12" width; fit into width of pan in the same manner, perpendicular to first sheet. Spray foil lined pan with non-stick cooking spray.

2.) Whisk to combine flour, salt and baking powder in medium bowl; set aside.

3.) Melt butter and chocolate in large heatproof bowl set over saucepan of almost-simmering water, stirring occasionally, until smooth. When chocolate mixture is completely smooth, remove bowl from saucepan and gradually whisk in sugar. Add eggs one at a time, whisking after each addition until thoroughly combined. Whisk in vanilla. Add flour mixture in three additions, folding with rubber spatula until batter is completely smooth and homogenous. Add pecans or walnuts.

4.) Transfer batter to prepared pan; using spatula, spread batter into corners of pan and smooth. Bake until toothpick inserted into center of brownies comes out with only a few moist crumbs attached, 30-35 minutes.

5.) Cool on wire rack to room temperature, about 2 hours, then remove brownies by lifting from pan by overhanging foil.

B.Erickson ©

Bill makes these brownies for his loving wife, Dina. They are Dina's absolute favorite, especially after Bill slaves over them.

## Mom's Brownies

4 eggs
2 C. sugar
1 1/3 C. Wesson Oil
4 Sq baking chocolate
2 tsp vanilla
2 C. flour
1 tsp baking powder
1 1/2 tsp salt
Bake 9x13 pan 350°   30-35 min.

B. Erickson ©

My mother never made box brownies when I was growing up. This is still my sister, Cathy's and my favorite brownie recipe.

# German Chocolate Cake Square

1 pkg (4 oz) Baker's German Chocolate 1/2 tsp salt
1 1/2 c sifted cake flour 1/3 cp butter
1 cp sugar 3/4 cp buttermilk
1/2 tsp baking soda 1 tsp vanilla
1/2 tsp baking powder 2 large eggs

Melt chocolate.
Sift flour with sugar, soda, powder, and salt.
Stir butter to soften.  Add flour mixture.  Add 1/2 cp buttermilk and
vanilla.  Beat 2 min.
Add melted chocolate, eggs and remaining buttermilk.  Beat 1 minute.
Bake in 9" square pan - lightly greased.
Bake 350° 40 min.

B.Erickson ©

Bonnie's recipe is so delicious it needs no frosting.

# Da Cake

8 oz. semi-sweet chocolate, chopped
8 oz. good quality bittersweet
　　chocolate, chopped
1 C unsalted butter

2 T liqueur (Kahlua or Grand Marnier)
9 large eggs, separated, whites
　　at room temp.
1 3/4 C sugar

Melt chocolates and butter in double boiler. Let mixture cool, stir in liqueur.
Beat egg yolks with sugar for 10 min. Stir chocolate mixture into egg yolk.
In separate bowl, with clean beaters, beat egg whites until barely stiff. Fold
chocolate mixture into egg whites in thirds. Turn batter into buttered and
floured 10" spring form pan, bake 350°, 25-30 min. It will be crisp on top, but
moist in center. Cool in pan, then refrigerate in pan, loosely covered, at least 4
hours. It will fall, and top will crack, but that's OK. To serve, remove side of
pan, and cut with a knife dipped in hot water. Serves 16. Great with fresh
raspberries and/or vanilla ice cream.

B. Erickson ©

Miriam gave this painting to Katie as it is Katie's family's favorite recipe. It has
become a family tradition at Christmas and her brother's birthday. Fondly known
as "Da Cake," it is rich and delicious as is, but ice cream and raspberries add the
crowning touch.

77

# Fruit Salad Cake

1 1/2 cups sugar
2 cups flour
2 tsp baking soda
1/2 tsp salt
2 eggs
14 oz can fruit cocktail

Preheat oven to 350 degrees. Beat eggs in medium bowl. Add everything except the flour and mix. Add flour and mix. Bake in 9 x 13 greased pan for 45 min.

Icing
3/4 cup white sugar
1/2 cup cream
1/2 cup butter
1 tsp vanilla extract

In a small pan, bring all ingredients (except vanilla) to a low boil. Add vanilla and remove from heat.

While cake is still hot, pierce holes all over with a fork. Pour icing mixture over cake. Serve warm with whipped cream.

B. ERICKSON ©

Susan gave this painting to her best friend, Lynne. When they were raising their children, they would often share family meals. This dessert was made so often, that finally their husbands would look forward to getting together as long as no one made the "Fruit Salad Cake!" Years later it's still a favorite for both Susan and Lynne.

# Maraschino Cherry Cake

1/3 cp shortening
1 cp sugar
2 eggs
2 cp flour
1/4 tsp salt
2 1/2 tsp baking powder
1/2 tsp vanilla
1/4 tsp almond extract
1/2 cp cherries - cut in small pieces
1/2 cp walnuts
2/3 cp milk

Cream shortening, add sugar gradually and cream until light. Add eggs and beat well. Add salt and baking powder to flour. (I mix a little flour with the cherries.) Add flour mixture alternately with milk, then flavorings and lastly cherries and nuts. Bake 350° about 1 hour.

Frosting: 1 cp confectioners sugar, small piece of butter, 1/4 tsp almond extract, cherry juice.

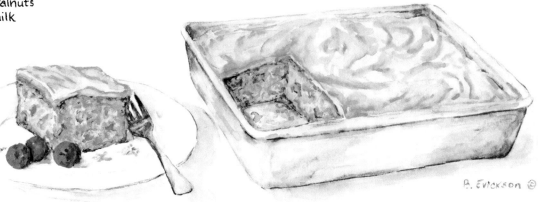

A. Erickson ©

Joyce's Mom made this cherry cake. We illustrated it being served just as she enjoyed it growing up - straight from the pan, which keeps it moist. When Joyce's sister was married, Joyce, her sister and their mom each made a layer of the wedding cake. Their mom made the Cherry Cake for the top layer. Joyce gave this painting to her sister for her sister's 25th anniversary.

*Danish Klejner*

3 eggs 1 cup sugar
½ teaspoon salt
1   "  Baking powder
1   "  vanilla
4 tablespoon milk
½ cups melted butter
        or margarine
3-4 cup flour

beat eggs + sugar
add milk + butter
vanilla
mix B.P. + salt with
flour.
then put together
work it well
use enough flour
to make a dough
to roll out
bake in deep fat

*the problem is simply to find out whether you can produce them faster than you can consume them.*

B. ERICKSON ©

This recipe, Danish Klejners, is difficult to read. Helen's Mother-in-law immigrated from Denmark and spoke broken English so we decided to copy the handwriting, including the phrase "bake in deep fat" instead of the word she didn't know – fry. We also used her antique bowl and one-handled rolling pin.

## Sugar'n Spice Cookies

Cream together 3/4 cup shortening and 1 cup sugar. Add 1 egg and 1/4 cup molasses. Sift together 2 cups flour, 2 tsp. soda, 1 tsp. cinnamon, and 1/4 tsp. each of salt, cloves, mace, nutmeg. Add dry ingredients to the creamed mixture.

Using the palms of your hands, form balls the size of small walnuts. Dip the balls into granulated sugar and place sugar side up about 2" apart on cookie sheet. Bake 9 or 10 min. in preheated 350° oven. They puff up, then crackle and fall.

Serve with a big, cold glass of Smiling Hill Farm Milk.

B. Erickson ©

Roger and Sally asked me to paint these cookies. Roger picked the recipe. The milk is from their dairy and tastes just like the milk I grew up with. We laugh that it took three batches of cookies to complete the painting because we kept eating the props!

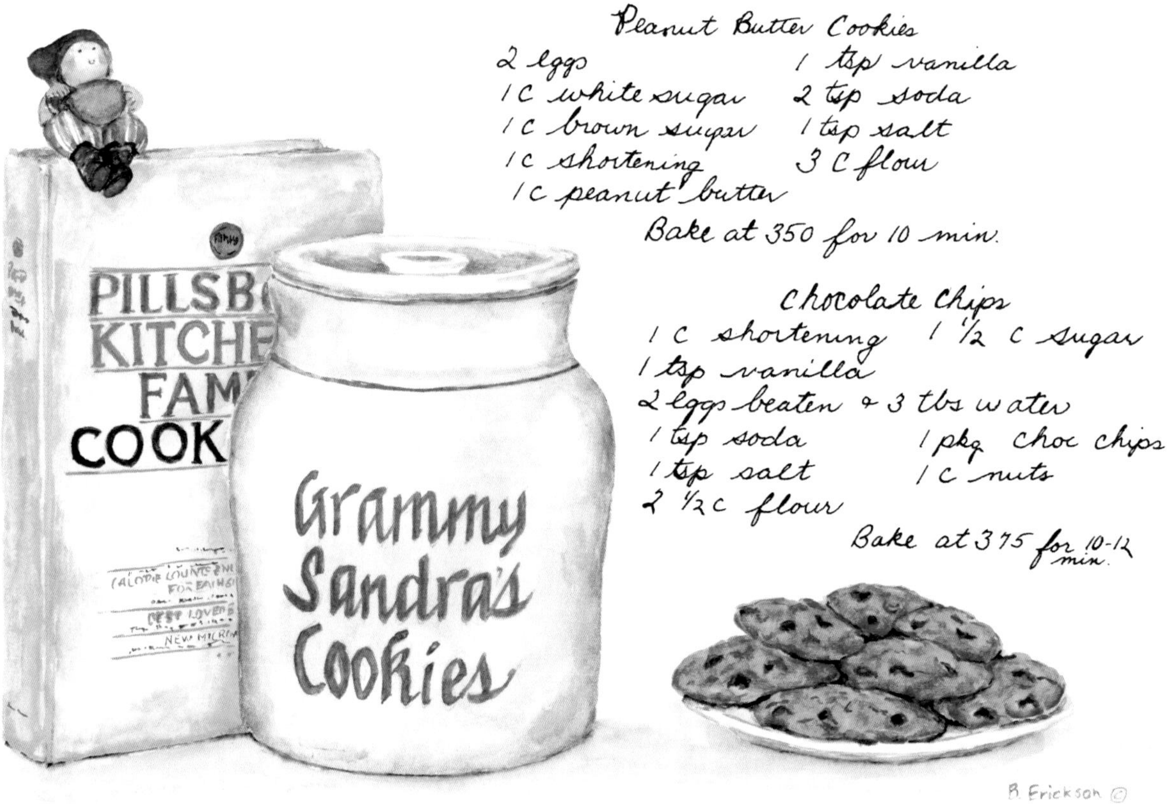

Peanut Butter Cookies
2 eggs
1 C white sugar
1 C brown sugar
1 C shortening
1 C peanut butter
1 tsp vanilla
2 tsp soda
1 tsp salt
3 C flour
Bake at 350 for 10 min.
Chocolate Chips
1 C shortening
1 ½ C sugar
1 tsp vanilla
2 eggs beaten & 3 tbs water
1 tsp soda
1 tsp salt
2 ½ C flour
1 pkg choc chips
1 C nuts
Bake at 375 for 10-12 min.
PILLSB
KITCHE
FAM
COOK
Grammy
Sandra's
Cookies
B. Erickson ©

Cheryl's Mom always kept this cookie jar full. The two recipes are from her Mom's favorite cookbook. The 'baking gnome' always sat on the windowsill watching over everyone in the kitchen. It now sits lovingly in Cheryl's kitchen.

# Chocolate Chip Cookies

1 cp butter

2 1/4 cp flour

1 t baking soda

1 t salt

1 cp packed brown sugar

1/2 cp granulated sugar

2 eggs

1 t vanilla

2 cps chocolate chips

Combine flour, baking soda and salt. Beat butter, both sugars and vanilla until fluffy. Add eggs one at a time. Gradually add dry ingredients until blended. Add chocolate chips. Bake 8-10 min. at 375°

D Erickson ©

The Toll House Cookie originated at Ruth Wakefield's Toll House Inn in Whitman, Massachusetts. I believe I read somewhere that one day she was late making dinner and didn't have time to melt the chocolate, so simply broke it up in pieces. It quickly became a very popular cookie. This is my mother's version.

# Celia's Old Fashioned Donuts

Mix:
1 cp sugar
1/4 cp oil
Add and beat:
2 eggs
1 tbsp vanilla
1 cp buttermilk

In sifter:
3 cp flour
1 3/4 tsp Bakewell
1 3/4 baking soda
1 1/4 tsp nutmeg
1 tsp salt
1/4 tsp ginger

Sift in flour plus rest.
Mix well and let set 3 hours or overnite in refridge.
Knead on board with flour.
Roll out and cut out with donut cutter.
Fry in Crisco in 9 inch fry pan.
Makes 32 donuts.

Celia makes these old fashioned donuts every day with the Maine product, Bakewell Cream. Most people in town know about Celia's donuts because she donates them to all the community activities. Since painting this recipe, I've met so many wonderful relatives of Celia's and each of them has a different story about Celia and her donuts. It's very rewarding.

# Rhoda Weston's Mandelbrot

### Yields: 48 pieces

3 large eggs
1 cup sugar
6 oz. corn oil
3/4 cp sliced or
   slivered almonds
3/4 cp golden raisins

2 tsp. almond extract
4 cups all-purpose flour
Cinnamon and sugar mixture
(more cinnamon than
commercial blend)

Preheat oven to 325°. Beat eggs, sugar and oil together in large mixing bowl. Add almonds, raisins and extract; mix well. Add flour; mix well and form into glossy ball. Divide ball into four quarters. Form each quarter into 8-in. length bar. Place two bars on cookie sheet lined with parchment. Sprinkle with cinnamon and sugar mixture. Repeat procedure with other two bars. Bake for 45 minutes. Cool slightly. While warm, slice each bar on the diagonal. Turn slices on their side with cinnamon and sugar mixture. Return to oven for 5 minutes or until lightly browned.

B. Erickson ©

This recipe appeared in a newspaper in New York about 60 years ago and it has been a favorite of the Weston family and friends ever since. Everyone always tells Rhoda that she better not show up without it! Rhoda's son, Evan always fights to get the "ends" and wishes his mom could just make a batch of ends. Known as Jewish biscotti, mandelbrot is the perfect way to end a meal.

# LEMON BARS

CRUST
2 cp flour
1/2 cp powdered sugar
1/2 lb margarine

FILLING
4 eggs
2 cp sugar
1/3 cp lemon juice
1/4 cp flour
1/2 t baking powder
1 t lemon zest

Combine ingredients for crust. Press mixture into 9x13 pan. Bake (350) for 25 min. While crust is baking, combine remaining ingredients. Remove crust from oven and pour filling over baked crust. Return to oven for 25 min. Remove, cool and sprinkle with powdered sugar. Store in airtight container up to two weeks.

B. Erickson©

This is my favorite lemon dessert, especially with the juicer my sister, Cathy gave me for Christmas.

# Lemon Meringue Pie

1/4 cp cornstarch
1/8 tsp salt
1 cp sugar
1 1/2 cp boiling water
6 tbsp lemon juice
1 tbsp lemon zest
3 egg yolks, beaten
1 tbsp butter

3 egg whites
6 tbsp sugar
1 tsp lemon juice

1 baked piecrust

Mix cornstarch, salt and sugar; add water, juice and zest. Cook until thickened, stirring constantly. Stir in beaten yolks and cook 1 min. longer. Blend in butter. Cool. Pour into baked pie shell. Beat whites to soft peaks. Add sugar gradually and continue beating until stiff. Add juice. Spread over cool filling and pastry. Bake 325° 12-18 min.

B. Erickson

This is my husband, Bob's favorite Pie.

## Granny's Jam

3 cups crushed Red Raspberries
5 1/2 cups sugar
1 box pectin

Crush berries, 1 cup at a time, with potato masher leaving bits of fruit. Accurate measure is important. Measure sugar in separate bowl, then stir into prepared fruit. Mix well, let stand 10 minutes; stir occasionally. Stir 1 box pectin and 3/4 cup water in small saucepan. Bring to boil, then continue to boil 1 minute, stirring constantly. Remove from heat. Stir pectin into fruit mixture. Stir constantly until sugar is completely dissolved and no longer grainy, about 3 minutes. Pour into prepared containers, leaving 1/2 inch space at top for expansion during freezing; cover. Makes about 7 cups.

Tom asked me to paint this for his mom and his young son, Anton. Granny makes the jam in these jars and sends them from Wisconsin to Maine for her grandson. When I delivered the painting, Anton was there. Tom asked him, "Is this is what Granny's Jam looks like?" His eyes lit up when he answered, "Yes."

88

## Rhubarb Crisp

**Topping:**
1 cup all purpose flour
1 cup lightly packed light brown sugar
1/2 cup old-fashioned oats
1/2 tsp ground cinnamon
1/4 tsp Kosher salt
8 Tbs cold unsalted butter cut into small pieces

**Filling:**
7 cups 1/3 inch thick sliced rhubarb (about 2 lbs)
1 cup lightly packed light brown sugar
1/4 cup cornstarch
1 Tbs fresh lemon juice
2 tsp finely grated lemon zest
1/4 tsp Kosher salt

Butter an 8x8 inch baking dish; preheat oven to 350°. In a food processor, combine dry ingredients, pulse several times. Add butter and pulse until mixture is texture of coarse meal, about 1 min.

Combine rhubarb, brown sugar, cornstarch, lemon juice, zest and salt in large bowl. Transfer rhubarb mixture to baking pan and sprinkle topping evenly over fruit; pan will be very full but will settle as it bakes. Strawberries may be added (adjust sugar accordingly)

Bake until topping is lightly browned, rhubarb is tender (probe in center with toothpick) and juices are bubbling thickly around edges, 45 to 60 minutes. Cool to room temp and allow juices to thicken, at least 1 hr. Serve with Edy's Vanilla Ice Cream.

B. Erickson ©

Jane asked me to paint this recipe for her son. Both Jane and her son, Bruce, love to garden and that includes growing rhubarb. She explained how her son is a good cook and this recipe is one he brought to the house that they all enjoyed.

# Strawberry Shortcake

2 cps Flour
3 tbsp Sugar
2 tsp Baking powder
1/2 tsp Salt
1/2 cp Shortening
1 Egg, beaten with
3/4 cp Whole milk
1 qt Strawberries
1 pt Whipping cream

Blend shortening into dry ingredients. Add milk gradually to make a soft dough. Pat on floured board to 3/4 inch thick. Cut with biscuit cutter and bake 400° for 15 minutes. Serve with fresh strawberries and whipped cream.

B. ERICKSON

June is strawberry month in Maine. For the best flavor, cut the strawberries a little ahead of time and let the juices blend.

# Teenie Bartell's Pecan Tarts

Great Grandmother (Mom)
Everyone called Mom the "Tart Lady"

1 stick butter
1 3 oz. Philadelphia cream cheese
1 cup flour
Mix above together and form into 24 little balls.
Shape by hand and form into small muffin tins
Place a few finely chopped nuts in bottom of tarts
Fill (almost to the top) with filling and top with
few more nuts. (Pecans are best, but walnuts
all right.)
Filling:
2 eggs (broken, but not beaten)
1 1/2 cup brown sugar
2 T melted butter
1 tsp. vanilla
Bake at 325° for 30 min. Cool in tins.

B. Erickson ©

Cheryl wants her niece to remember her Great Grandmother, Teenie Bartell. We used Mom's bowl and tart pan. They are so easy and delicious, that this is now one of my favorite company desserts.

# Turtle Popcorn

16 cp popcorn, fresh popped, unsalted
8 oz dark baking chocolate or white chocolate
1 tsp salt
1 tsp shortening
1 cp sugar
1 cp light corn syrup
1 cp cream
1 lb plus 2 tsp butter

Coat 11 x 17 baking pan w/ 2 tsp butter. Toss popcorn & salt together. Spread evenly in baking pan (set aside). Melt chocolate & shortening in double boiler, stirring occasionally (set aside and keep warm). Combine and simmer sugar, corn syrup, cream and butter in medium saucepan and bring to 249 f (firm-ball stage). Immediately remove from heat and pour caramel over popcorn in fat ribbons. Pour chocolate in fat ribbons over popcorn, taking care not to completely cover caramel. Cool, then break into pieces. Store in airtight container.

B. Erickson ©

Susan wanted to do something nice for her children. This is their special recipe. They also collect antiques so we used a selection of antiques in the painting.

# Nana's Monkey Bread

James Lisa Evan Jared
Riley Cam Eric Liz
Lauren Jeffrey Shannon
Sean Dylan Annie

4 packages biscuits
2 teaspoons cinnamon
1 cup sugar

3/4 cup butter
1/2 cup brown sugar
6 cups Nana's Love

Mix 1 tsp of cinnamon with 1/2 cup of sugar. Quarter the biscuits and coat with mixture. Melt together butter, brown sugar, the rest of sugar and cinnamon along with 6 heaping cups of Nana's Love. Place coated biscuit pieces in a greased bundt pan. Pour melted mixture over top. Bake at 350 for 30 minutes. Invert onto platter and enjoy!

* For best results think of Nana the whole time it's baking!

B.Erickson ©

Nana made a big production with her grandchildren when making Monkey Bread together. Little hands always had fun shaking the sugar and dough in a plastic bag. Today it's Nana's daughter who carries on the tradition and this is her cup and plate. The six cups of love represent Nana's six children. The names coming out of the measuring cup are all of her grandchildren.

93

# Pumpkin Pie

1 cp sugar
½ tsp salt
1 tbsp cornstarch
½ tsp cinnamon
½ tsp ginger
½ tsp nutmeg

1 can prepared pumpkin
2 eggs, beaten
1 ½ tbsp butter, melted
⅛ cp molasses
1- 12 oz can evaporated milk
1 prepared pie crust

Sift together sugar, cornstarch, salt cinnamon, ginger and nutmeg. Mix with prepared pumpkin. Add eggs, melted butter, molasses and evaporated milk. Pour contents into prepared pie crust. Bake at 450° for 15 min. Reduce temperature to 350° and bake for additional 50 minutes.

There is nothing more fun than painting a bright orange pumpkin. And then to enjoy the pie after? It doesn't get much better than that.

94

### Damariscotta Pumpkinfest Whoopie Pies
#### October 2010

| | |
|---|---|
| 1 c sugar | 3/4 c unsalted butter |
| 1 c maple sugar | 2 1/2 c confectioners' |
| 1 c melted butter | sugar, sifted |
| 3 eggs | 1 t cinnamon |
| 2 c cooked | 1/4 t nutmeg, |
| puréed pumpkin | freshly grated |
| 2 c flour | pinch of salt |
| 1/2 t salt | 1 T vanilla extract |
| 1/2 t baking powder | 2 T Maine maple syrup |
| 1 t baking soda | 2 t fresh lemon juice |
| 2 t cinnamon | 2 egg whites |
| 1 t ground nutmeg | |

Bake 350 F, 10-14 min
Until golden brown and springy

For complete directions, see:
Delicious Maine Desserts
By Cynthia Finnemore Simonds

B. Erickson ©

The Damariscotta Pumpkinfest is held each October, and features the unequaled paddleboat and motorized Pumpkinboat 'Regatta', pumpkin chunkers and catapaulters, a 150' pumpkin drop, a parade down Main Street past giant carved pumpkins, as well as family-oriented games & activities. The recipe is from TV chef of 'Fresh and Flavorful' and cookbook author, Cynthia Finnemore Simonds. The Whoopie Pies are simply delicious!

# Whoopie Pies

1 cp sugar
2 cp flour
1 1/4 tsp soda
1/2 tsp salt
5 tbsp cocoa
6 tbsp shortening
1 cp milk
1 tsp vanilla
1 egg

Frosting:
6 tbsp marshmallow fluff
3/4 cp shortening
3/4 cp confectionary sugar
1 tsp vanilla
A little milk

Sift dry ingredients. Mix in wet
ingredients until creamy. Spoon a
tablespoon of batter on ungreased pan
Bake 350°, 10 min. Frost generously.
Add secret ingredient. (LOVE)

B. ERICKSON ©

Whoopie Pies are a Maine Dessert. This recipe was painted for my cousin, Charlie. He asked that they be coming out of the fluff container. As I set it up, I looked at it and wondered what to do next. My aunt, Ginny who is deceased, was also an artist. I have always felt that she took over and set up the remaining whoopie pies. They seem to be happy and smiling and that's how I always felt when I was with her.